W9-ANH-530

DISCARD

Hebron Public Library
201 W. Sigler Street
PORTER COUNTY
LIBRARY SYSTEM
Hebron, IN 46341

NEIGHBORHOOD HELPERS

Television Reporters

PORTER COUNTY LIBRARY

BY DAVE CUPP AND CECILIA MINDEN

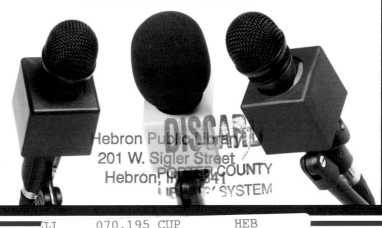

Hebron Public Library
201 W. Sigler Street
Hebron, IN 46341

DISCARD

PORTER COUNTY
LIBRARY SYSTEM

JJ   070.195 CUP   HEB
Cupp, Dave.
Television reporters /
33410009102783

NOV 14 2006

The Child's World®

Content Adviser:
Tom Muston, News Anchor,
KCNC-TV (CBS),
Highlands Ranch, Colorado

Published in the United States of America by The Child's World®
PO Box 326
Chanhassen, MN 55317-0326
800-599-READ
www.childsworld.com

Acknowledgements

The Child's World®: Mary Berendes, Publishing Director

Editorial Directions, Inc.: E. Russell Primm, Editorial Director; Katie Marsico, Managing Editor and
Line Editor; Judith Shiffer, Assistant Editor; Caroline Wood, Editorial Assistant; Susan Hindman,
Copy Editor; Wendy Mead, Proofreader; Mike Helenthal, Rory Mabin, and Caroline Wood, Fact
Checkers; Tim Griffin/IndexServ, Indexer; Cian Loughlin O'Day, Photo Researcher; Linda S. Koutris,
Photo Selector

The Design Lab: Kathleen Petelinsek, Design and Art Production

Photographs ©: Cover: left—Digital Vision/Punchstock, right/frontispiece—Photodisc/Getty Images.
Interior: 4, 6, 17—Photodisc/Getty Images; 5—Stockbyte/Getty Images; 7—Dave Cupp; 8-9—Mark
Harmel/Taxi/Getty Images; 11—Ken Fisher/Stone/Getty Images; 12—Jim Carpenter; 14-15—David
Butow/Corbis Saba; 19—Judy Beyer; 20-21—Enigma/Alamy Images; 22-23—Greg Pease/Stone/
Getty Images; 24—Popperfoto/Alamy Images; 26-27, 29—Michael Krasowitz/Taxi/Getty Images.

Copyright © 2006 by The Child's World®. All rights reserved. No part of this book may be reproduced
or utilized in any form or by any means without written permission from the publisher.

Library of Congress Cataloging-in-Publication Data
Cupp, Dave.
 Television reporters / by Dave Cupp and Cecilia Minden.
   p. cm.
 ISBN 1-59296-570-9 (library bound : alk. paper)
1. Television broadcasting of news—Vocational guidance—Juvenile literature. 2. Reporters and
reporting-Vocational guidance—Juvenile literature. I. Minden, Cecilia. II. Cupp, Dave. III. Title.
 PN4784.T4C87 2006
 070.1'95-dc22   2005026221

TABLE OF CONTENTS

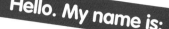

Hello. My name is:

Annika

Hello. My name is Annika. Many people live and work in my neighborhood. Each of them helps the neighborhood in different ways.

I thought of all the things I like to do. I like to search the computer and find interesting facts. I like to share what I've learned with my friends. I like talking to people.

How could I help my neighborhood when I grow up?

TV news reports began in the early 1940s. They were once a day and lasted fifteen minutes. These reports became longer and more detailed in the mid-1950s. Videotape allowed reporters to cover more stories. Today, Americans rely on TV reporters for news.

I COULD BE A TV REPORTER!

Television (TV) reporters are good at reading and writing. They search for information and interesting facts. They help people in the neighborhood share their stories.

Best of all, they get to be on TV!

TV reporters read the news on camera. Do you like being on camera?

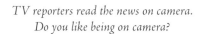

LEARN ABOUT THIS NEIGHBORHOOD HELPER!

The best way to learn is to ask questions. Words such as *who, what, where, when,* and *why* will help me learn about being a TV reporter.

Asking a TV reporter questions will help you learn more about his job.

Where Can I Learn More?

The National Association of Broadcasters
1771 N Street NW
Washington, DC 20036

Radio-Television News Directors Association
1600 K Street NW
Suite 700
Washington, DC 20006

How Can
I Explore
This Job?

Does your community have a local TV station? Call and ask if you can visit. You might even get a tour of the newsroom! Ask any reporters you meet what they like best about their job.

WHO CAN BECOME A TV REPORTER?

Girls and boys who are good at writing, speaking, and listening might want to become TV reporters. A good TV reporter also needs to know how to ask questions. A TV reporter is not shy!

TV reporters are important helpers in the neighborhood. They help people find out what is going on around them.

TV reporters help people learn about important events in their neighborhood.

MEET A TV REPORTER!

This is Dana Hackett. Dana is a TV
reporter at station WVIR-TV/DT
in Charlottesville, Virginia. When she
is not reporting the news, she likes to
dance, play her flute, travel, and root for
her favorite sports teams.

Dana reports the news in Charlottesville.

How Many TV Reporters Are There?

About 66,000 people work as news reporters. About 16,500 work in radio and TV broadcasting.

How Much School Will I Need?

TV reporters usually have a four-year college degree. Most study journalism in college.

WHERE CAN I LEARN TO BE A TV REPORTER?

Most TV reporters go to college. Dana went to the University of North Carolina. She learned to gather facts and write well. She also took classes in history, science, and math. A TV reporter needs to know about many different things.

Most TV reporters take a variety of classes in college.

Laptop computer

Microphone

Satellite videophones

Teleprompter

Video camera and video editing equipment

microphone (MYE-kruh-fone) an instrument that uses electric currents to make sound louder

teleprompter (TEH-luh-prohmp-tuhr) a special camera that people can read off of while reporting the news or giving a speech

WHAT DOES A TV REPORTER NEED TO DO HER JOB?

Dana and her crew need video cameras to record events. This allows the people watching television to see what is happening in the story. Dana also needs a **microphone** so people can hear what she has to say.

Dana needs to talk to the audience when she shares the news. She does this by looking into a **teleprompter.** The teleprompter allows Dana to look at the audience and read the news at the same time!

What Clothes Will I Wear?

For men:
Suit and tie

For women:
Blazer and blouse
Skirt or slacks

A newsroom is often a large room. Most people in the newsroom work quickly. They need to finish their stories on time. They use computers and often spend a lot of time on the telephone. TV reporters might work any time of day or night. They need to cover stories as they are happening. TV reporters often travel. They sometimes even have to work in dangerous situations.

WHERE DOES A TV REPORTER WORK?

Dana's day usually starts with a meeting in the newsroom in Charlottesville. This is where stories are assigned. She spends time in an office making phone calls or checking facts on the computer. Then Dana goes into Charlottesville's different neighborhoods to interview people. Finally, she comes back to the newsroom to write her story. TV reporters have to

TV reporters often have to make phone calls and do research on the computer to prepare for a story.

be quick because the stories are often due at the end of the day!

Dana's job takes her to many different places in Charlottesville. One day she may write a story about a fire. Another day she may write a story about a local election. What an exciting job!

TV reporters cover a variety of events, including local fires.

How Much Money Will I Make?

Most TV reporters make between $17,000 and $70,000 per year.

What Other Jobs Might I Enjoy?

Camera operator

Meteorologist

News director

Newspaper reporter

Radio reporter

Sports announcer

Videographer

WHO WORKS WITH TV REPORTERS?

Many people work at WVIR-TV with Dana. They all come together every day to make sure the news gets to people in Charlottesville. Many people work behind the camera. One important person behind the camera is the producer. The producer runs the whole show.

Producers play an important role at TV stations.

WHEN DOES A TV REPORTER GET TO TRAVEL?

Sometimes TV reporters get to travel to other countries. TV reporters from around the world cover big events such as the Olympics. Each TV reporter at a major event may come from a different country and speak a different language. They are all working quickly to create **accurate** news stories!

Reporters from around the world cover major events such as the Olympics.

How Might My Job Change?

TV reporters often start at a small, local TV station. They usually work as a researcher or production assistant. Some work as reporters behind the scenes. TV reporters eventually gain more experience and go on to report more stories in front of a camera. They sometimes leave smaller stations to take jobs at larger ones.

accurate (AK-yuh-rut) completely correct

I WANT TO BE A TV REPORTER!

I think being a TV reporter would be a great way to be a neighborhood helper. Someday you may see me on the evening news!

Smile into the camera! Maybe one day you'll help your neighborhood by reporting the news!

Is This Job Growing?

The need for TV reporters will grow more slowly than other jobs.

I Didn't Know That!

The most important award given to TV reporters is the Alfred I. DuPont-Columbia University Award. This award is given every year to TV and radio reporters with the best news stories.

WHY DON'T YOU TRY BEING A TV REPORTER?

Do you think you would like to be a TV reporter? Read this list of facts.

+ First pig builds home.
+ Wolf comes along and blows it down.
+ Second pig builds home.
+ Wolf comes along and blows it down.
+ Third pig builds home.
+ Wolf cannot blow down the house.
+ Wolf tries to get in through chimney.
+ Pig tricks wolf.

* House and pig are saved.

Talk to your friends to see if they know anything about what happened. Do you have enough facts to write a news story? What pictures could you draw to help tell the story? Now write the story. Then read the story to your friends just like a real TV reporter would read to an audience.

Do you have what it takes to be a TV reporter? Good TV reporters know how to gather information and share it in an interesting way.

HOW TO LEARN MORE ABOUT TV REPORTERS

BOOKS

Byrum, R. T. *Television*. San Diego: Lucent Books, 2005.

Davis, Gary. *Working at a TV Station*. Danbury, Conn.: Children's Press, 1999.

Hayward, Linda. *A Day in the Life of a TV Reporter*. New York: Dorling Kindersley, 2001.

Nagle, Jeanne M. *Careers in Television*. New York: Rosen Publishing Group, 2001.

WEB SITES

Visit our home page for lots of links about
TV reporters:
http://www.childsworld.com/links

Note to Parents, Teachers, and Librarians:

We routinely check our Web links to make sure they're
safe, active sites—so encourage your readers to check
them out!

ABOUT THE AUTHORS:

Dave Cupp was the News Director and Anchor for WVIR for twenty-five years. He is now an Assistant Professor in the School of Journalism and Mass Communication at the University of North Carolina.

Dr. Cecilia Minden is a university professor and reading specialist with classroom and administrative experience in grades K–12. She is the author of many books for early readers. Cecilia and her husband Dave Cupp live in North Carolina. She earned her PhD in reading education from the University of Virginia.

INDEX